SERMONS & HOMILIES

SERMONS & HOMILIES

RADBOUD OF UTRECHT

Copyright 2025 by Dalcassian Press

All rights reserved. No part of this book may be reproduced in any manner whatsoever without written permission except in the case of brief quotations embodied in critical articles and reviews.

No part of this publication may be reproduced, distributed, or transmitted in any form or by any means, including photocopying, recording, or other electronic or mechanical methods, without the prior written permission of the publisher, except in the case of brief quotations embodied in critical reviews and certain other non-commercial uses permitted by copyright law. For permission request, write to Dalcassian Press at admin@thescriptoriumproject.com

Translator: Curtin, D.P. (1985-)

ISBN: 979-8-3492-6742-0 (Paperback)
ISBN: 979-8-3492-6741-3 (eBook)
Library of Congress Control Number:

Printed by Ingram Content Group, 1 Ingram Blvd, La Vergne, Tennessee
First Printing 2025, Dalcassian Press, Wilmington, DE

This work is part of a series produced in association with the Scriptorium Project and its community of scholars and translators.
Please visit our website at: www.thescriptoriumproject.com

LATIN TEXT

SERMO S. RADBODI DE S. SWITBERTO.

1. Acturi, fratres charissimi, diem nostrae specialis jucunditatis, in qua patroni nostri beatissimi Switberti sancta admodum commemoratio facienda est, oportet nos paratos esse ad omne opus bonum, promptosque habere animos; primo quidem ad audienda legis divinae mandata, postmodum vero ut, quantum possumus, ea factis exsequi studeamus, et sic demum alios docere possimus. Hoc enim fecit Dominus noster Jesus Christus, de quo ita scriptum est: Coepit Jesus facere et docere (Act. I, 1). Alioquin irrita et inanis nostra erit doctrina, si ea quae diximus, nihil agendo destruamus. Nam quid prodest alicui, si bene audiat, et male agat? aut quid proficit illi, si alii viam pedum ostendat, ipse autem in via morum errare non desinat? Nos igitur vestigia Redemptoris nostri sequentes, quaelibet bona libentissime audiamus; audita vero dignis actibus compleamus, et sic per ordinem ad instruendos proximos accedentes, consulamus eis rerum bonarum doctrinis pariter et exemplis. Hoc ergo ut sive dilatione fieri possit, revocanda sunt nobis ad memoriam Patris nostri, de quo supra diximus, opera: qui in omnibus quae docuit, prius a semetipso auditoribus suis exemplum dedit, neque unquam in Ecclesia a liud faciendum dixit quam in quo ipse faciendo praecessit. Verum ut se imitari volentibus hoc quoque manifestum fiat, facta ejus Deo placita, omnique audienti satis necessaria in publico recitentur, quatenus ex eisdem plebs Christi aedificationem accipiat, ac de tanti viri gloriosis precibus semper gratulabunda existat.

Sed quia nobis quaedam sunt occulta quae eum fecisse post Deum sola novit antiquitas: quippe qui ab Anglorum provincia in nostros fines venisse probatur, scripta venerabilis Bedae presbyteri proferantur in medium, qui in Regestis Anglorum, inter caetera sic de hoc sanctissimo viro scriptum relinquit.

2. Tempore B. Willibrodi Trajectensis episcopi, fratres, qui erant in Fresia verbi ministerio mancipati, elegerunt ex suo numero virum modestum moribus et mansuetum corde, Switbertum, qui eis ordinaretur antistes. Quem ad Britanniam destinatum, ad petitionem eorum ordinavit reverendissimus Wilfrid episcopus qui, tum forte patria pulsus, in Merciorum regionibus exsulabat. Non enim eo tempore habebat episcopum Cantia, defuncto quidem Theodoro, sed necdum Berthwaldo successore ejus, qui trans mare ordinandus ierat, ad sedem episcopatus sui reverso. Qui videlicet Switbrecht, accepto episcopatu, de Britannia regressus, non multo post ad gentem Boructuariorum secessit, ac multos eorum praedicando ad viam veritatis perduxit. Sed expugnatis non longo post tempore Boructuariis, a gente antiquorum Saxonum dispersi sunt quolibet hi qui verbum receperant. Ipse antistes cum quibusdam Pippinum petiit qui, interpellante Blithrude conjuge sua, dedit ei locum mansionis in insula Rheni, quae lingua illorum vocatur in littore. In qua ipse constructo monasterio, quod hactenus haeredes possident ejus, aliquandiu continentissimam gessit vitam, ibique clausit ultimum diem.

3. Haec igitur, quae superius de hoc sanctissimo viro digesta sunt, Bedam commemorasse neminem ambigere credimus, nisi forte quempiam talem, qui aliis vacans negotiis librum illum, ubi ea scripta sunt, aut non legit, aut certe legendo neglexit. Caeterum nos nequaquam dubitare debemus, virum istum in omnibus Christianae religionis studiis fuisse exercitatum, utpote qui inter tam pretiosas Ecclesiae Dei lucernas, quae his diebus sive in Anglorum, sive in Galliarum gente mirifice coruscabant, ovium Christi pastor a sacratissimis ipsis ordinari promeruit. Nam nisi esset pastorali exercitio pleniter instructus, nullo modo ejus custodiae, tantae gregis Christi copiae crederentur. Porro nisi esset miles quodammodo veteranus, et in agone martyrii fortis et imperterritus, nequaquam in acie Christi summus tribunus, nequaquam primipilus legis divinae constitueretur exercitus. Verum his allegorice praelibatis, moraliter quoque nos aperire oportet quae sint exercitia, quibus inexpugnabilem istum militem praeclarum fuisse non dubitamus. Quod quidem in Pastoralibus

primo est demonstrandum, in quibus sive leo saeviens, sive lupus insidians, non modicum Christi ovibus detrimentum important: ubi si pastor pervigil aut insidias caverit, aut rapinam fortiter resistendo excusserit, salvo grege ad caulas Dominicas remeabit. Si autem in quotidiano praecinctu positus arma nunquam deposuerit, sed vel de castris hostem repulerit, vel in campo aperte dimicans rite triumphaverit, intra sanctae civitatis moenia post haec tutissime imperabit.

4. Quae nimirum utroque beatissimum Switbertum fecisse non ignoramus. Nam dum in Ecclesia praesulatus officium gerens, fratres suos sive a deceptoriis persuasionibus retraheret, sive a contentionibus publicis revocaret, quasi leonem ferocissimum, et quasi lupum callidissimum, a grege Dominico excludebat. Cum vero aut regum potentia pressos, aut qualibet principum crudelitate vexatos gladio verbi Dei scutoque fidei a tyrannica persecutione defenderet, profecto tanquam dux egregius milites suos ad castra incolumes reducebat. Itaque si nosse desideras quae fuerint nostri hujus ducis in quotidianis congressibus arma, non ea fabrefacta, sed plane spiritualia cognosce. Neque enim erat ille oneratus ferro, sed potius fide, spe et charitate praecinctus; fundam David cum suo lapide tenens, et terribilem Philistaeum in fronte percutiens, omnemque Israelem a periculo mortis eripiens. Porro autem ne existimes illum hujusmodi arma unquam deponere esse solitum, isdem erat in pace ornatus quibus in bello stabat armatus. Semper erat humilis, semper mansuetus, et mitis, patiens in adversis, modestus in prosperis.

5. Erat quoque in pudicitia splendidus, in abstinentia strenuus, in vigiliis sobrius, in oratione stabilissimus. In judicio perorabat aequaliter, non personaliter; in compassione miserabatur humaniter, non tenaciter; alienorum non erat appetitor, sed propriorum largissimus erogator; vitium in homine acriter persequebatur, hominem vero familiariter amplectebatur. Sermo ejus ut mel dulcis, praedicatio ejus admodum delectabilis, convivium ejus spiritualibus ferculis plenum, contubernium ejus angelicum; mala omnia tanquam venena mortifera respuebat; bona omnia tanquam paradisi aromata diligebat.

Postremo si velut quemdam epilogum facere volueris; totus ille erat perfectus, et totus erat Deo plenus. Haec erant, fratres, patroni nostri beatissimi Switberti in adversis et prosperis arma: cum his in omni agone dimicabat, ac semper et ubique vincebat. Non enim erat illi colluctatio adversus carnem et sanguinem, sed adversus principes et potestates, adversus mundi rectores tenebrarum harum, contra spiritualia nequitiae in coelestibus.

6. Agamus ergo gratias omnipotenti Deo in die solemnitatis hujus sacrosancti antistitis, orantes simul et postulantes ut, cujus vitam gloriosam praedicamus in terris, ejus patrocinio perfrui mereamur in coelis. Amen.

SERMO RADBODI DE VITA S. VIRGINIS CHRISTI AMELBERGAE.

1. Quotiescunque, dilectissimi fratres, sanctorum Dei memoriam ad laudem et gloriam nominis ipsius agimus, toties a peccatorum nostrorum sepulcris resurgimus. Revivescit enim tunc quodammodo fides nostra, et rediviva innovatur dulcedine vox nostra per officia labiorum nostrorum, ac per hoc sit in nobis quod dicit Apostolus: Renovamini spiritu mentis vestrae, et induite novum hominem (Ephes. IV, 23). Quid namque est aliud male mori, in sepulcro, ac jacendo fetere, nisi peccatorum sordibus inquinari? Et quid aliud est ab hoc tumulo resurgere, nisi per confessionem et poenitentiam ad vitam, qui Christus est, redire? Habemus sane hujusmodi mortis plurima in Scripturis exempla, quae illos solet mortuos appellare, qui nunquam volunt a peccatis resipiscere; sicut est illud in Evangelio: Sinite mortuos sepelire mortuos suos (Luc. IX, 6). Neque enim ii qui corpora sepeliebant corporaliter mortui erant; sed cum essent scelerati, ac propterea mortui, sepeliebant eos quos mors corporis a vita subtraxit. Quocirca nos quoque mortis hujus detrimenta caveamus; quinimo de sepulcris vitiorum cito per gratiam Christi resurgere festinemus, ut cum ipso in aeterna beatitudine vivere mereamur.

2. Itaque laudemus Dominum Deum nostrum in sanctis suis, eosdemque vicissim collaudemus et honoremus in ipso, quando quidem Deo et sanctis ejus servire, vere est vivere, atque in hoc omni tempore permanere, prudenter est laqueos delictorum devitare. Ecce autem occurrit nobis hodierna die hujus rei aptissimum tempus, in quo paradoxae virginis Amalbergae memorabilem vitam annua festivitate recolimus, quae in hac peregrinatione Deo et hominibus gratissima exstitit, tum splendore geminae pulchritudinis, tum etiam merito pudicitiae virginalis. Haec, cum esset primis orta natalibus et propter nimium corporis decorem omnibus amabilis, elegit se ornare virtutum gemmis potius quam vestibus pretiosis, vilemque se et despicabilem statuit humanis ostendere oculis, quo pretiosa atque honestissima conspectibus appareret divinis. Non auro utebatur aut margaritis, quia sciebat Christum sponsum suum non iis fuisse usum in terris; non purpuram diligebat aut byssum, quoniam non ignorabat propter hujusmodi multos demergi in abyssum. Non delectabatur rumusculis frequentiae popularis, quia secretum locum noverat esse opportunum [amicum] moeroris.

3. Porro autem, iis contemptis, longe aliter factitabat; nam, pro cognatis et amicis saeculi, diligebat pauperes Christi; pro auro atque margaritis, ornabatur sententiis doctrinae spiritualis; pro byssinis purpureisque vestibus, cinere et silicio utebatur; pro frequentia populari, quam penitus respuebat, in excubiis templorum Domini, circa sacra altaria orando et vigilando jugiter morabatur. Verum quomodo et quali ordine ad tantam disciplinae coelestis pervenerit summam non est silentio transeundum propter exemplum bonum, et propter meritorum ejus dignum narratione praeconium. Erat quippe haec pudicissima puella in haereditate patrum suorum temporibus Francorum principum, quos quidem a Carolo Magno Carolidas possumus appellare, qui, ob multiplices victorias et admittenda in Christiana religione studia, hic solus inter caeteros vocabulum promeruit, ut merito magnus et optimus diceretur.

4. Horum, ut dictum est, in diebus sancta et Deo placita virgo Amelberga, defunctis jam parentibus, in possessione, quae ei secus

Scaldam fluvium latissima ex progenitorum successione provenerat, cum unico fratre suo religiosissime commanebat, jejuniis et orationibus serviens die ac nocte, eleemosynasque plurimas et largissimas faciens cum maxima hilaritate, habens semper in memoria illud apostolicum: Hilarem datorem diligit Deus (II Cor. IX, 7). Cumque esset speciosissima usque adeo ut reliquas omnes sua pulchritudine superaret, propter honestissimi corporis praerogativam pene incurrit pudicitiae detrimentum. Nam cum ejus opinio ad regem provinciae, Carolum videlicet, tunc temporis pervenisset, is, ejus amore continuo captus, coepit cum illa indesinenter de nuptiis per internuntios agere. Postquam vero sensit voluntatem suam a beata virgine, quae se meliori sponso, id est Christo, devoverat, omnimodis reprobari, quod blandimentis et potestate regia non valuit per insidias et quaedam latrocinia clanculo nisus est attentare. At illa contra haec omnia orationum clypeos et coelestis armaturae frameas ostendebat.

5. Quadam vero die, cum beatissima puella inter domesticos parietes sola resideret, psalmosque more solito caneret, puer familiaris repente per posticum irruit, proclamans et annuntians regem cum satellitibus suis adesse prae foribus. Tunc ipsa, nihil sui oblita, oratorium, quod domui adhaerebat, celeri cursu ingressa est, ubi se illico cum gemitu et lacrymis ad orationem prostravit, flebili voce obsecrans, ut eam Dominus de imminenti periculo liberaret. Tum vero rex, nimium temerarius, post eam in oratorium intrans, coepit illi multis adulationibus blandiri, honoresque promittere temporales, quo vel suis eam persuasionibus acquiescere faceret. Verum illa sponsum quem elegerat nullo modo derelinquere volens, jacebat immobilis, et ita solo defixa ac si quibuslibet radicibus implicita teneretur. Postquam autem rex cuncta blandimenta (vaniloquia) adhibuit, nihilque se proficere vidit, regiam auctoritatem vertit in saevissimam tyrannidem, arreptaque ejus manu violenter illam foras trahere conabatur. Sed cum etiam ita nullus eum sequeretur effectus, tandem puellae brachium fortiter excutiens, summaque vi torquens, fracto virginalis humeri osse quasi qui se vindicasset, abscessit.

6. Tunc illa, ut erat tenerrima, ob vulneris sui gravissimum dolorem, coram Domino aliquantulum quidem flevit; tandiu autem oravit, donec sponsus suus Christus adesset, eamque sanitate integra restauraret. Ex illa autem die nullum saecularem passa est amplius amatorem, sed libere in sponsi sui Domini nostri Jesu Christi dilectione permansit. O felix commercium! O nimium prudens electio, ubi rex terrae pro Creatore coeli et terrae contemnitur, ubi Deus pro homine adamatur, ubi pro luto isto coelestes divitiae conquiruntur! O beatissima virgo, si multum tibi sublimitas generis obfuit, aut multo magis tua spontanea dejectio, et carnis propter Deum contritio posuit? Si splendor tuae pulchritudinis periculum incurrit, et contemptus regiae majestatis perenni te gloria coronavit. Si ad horam passio contristavit, at tibi inde contubernium martyrum et requies sempiterna provenit. Ecce nunc omnibus quae in hac vita desiderasti perfrueris, quoniam rex regum et Dominus dominantium concupivit speciem tuam, tuque, o augustissima regina, assistis a dextris ejus in vestitu deaurato circumdata varietate.

7. Nunc igitur in te fides, spes, charitas fulgent, humilitas regnat, patientia triumphat, virginitas candet, pudicitia nitet, prudentia discernit, temperantia moderatur, fortitudo superat, justitia judicat, atque, ut epilogum faciamus, virtutum omnium in te et a te militia continetur. Quamobrem in aeterna beatitudine bona ineffabilia, non solum beatissimis oculis vides, et felicissimis manibus tenes, verum etiam reliqui sensus eadem felicitate fruuntur. Nam et beatis auribus coeleste organum audis, et laeto ore novum canticum canis, et venerandis naribus perennes modo delicias odoras. Itaque non erit ulterius quod tibi sollicitudinem pariat, vel quod anxietatem importet. Habes quippe gaudium absque tristitia, delectationem absque fastidio, securitatem absque formidine, pacem absque dissensione, dulcedinem absque amaritudine, satietatem absque defectione. Lux tibi sine tenebris lucet, munditia sine inquinamento resplendet; totam habes requiem, totam possides vitam, quae nec lassitudinem pateris, nec morti succumbis.

8. Quid ergo melius? quid jucundius? Opes terrenas aut fortunae rota subtrahit, aut conditio mortalitatis extorquet; thesauros vero coelestes ipsa sui perpetuitas oppido concupiscibiles facit. Hos tu, o beatissima virgo, cum angelis, propter caelibem tuam vitam: cum apostolis, propter fidem catholicam; cum martyribus, propter passionis constantiam; cum confessoribus, propter innocentiam sanctam; cum virginibus, propter specialem corporis et animae pudicitiam, vere nunc, patriam tuam post limina, repetens, haereditario jure participas, et gloriaris in sponso tuo Jesu Christo Domino nostro: per quem te oramus ac suppliciter petimus, ut pro nobis apud ipsum intercedere non desistas, qui te in hac mortalitate ita roboravit, ut regem terrenum castitatis gloria vinceres, et infernorum principem diabolum sanctitate praecipua superares, auxiliante ipso, qui cum Patre et Spiritu sancto gloriatur Deus, per omnia saecula saeculorum. Amen.

HOMILIA S. RADBODI DE SANCTO LEBWINO.

Saepe contingit, fratres charissimi, ut inter epulas grata sit convivantibus fabulosa narratio, et oppressum cibis carnalibus animum quaelibet figmentorum persequatur esuries, dumque sui oblita mens, ad tempus ob repletionem corporis obsonium spirituale fastidit, magis appetat species vanitatum, quibus aures carnis oblectet quam doctrinae coelestis dulcedinem, qua nauseantem animam vera et perpetua suavitate reficiat. Verum nobis in praesenti lectione multo aliter evenire, laetamur, qui quanto hanc solemnius aure carnis percipimus, tanto eam avidius in eo edamus, atque idipsum quod sumimus post venerandam esuriem satietatis opulentiam, post felicem satietatem, redivivam esuriem in nobis creare non dubitamus. Itaque, ut manifestius eluceat, quae (ut dicitur) cupedia spiritualibus famelicis hoc narrationis genere promittantur, ponantur jam super coelestem mensam fercula deliciis omnibus hujus saeculi gratiora, ex quibus suavissimas vitae perennis epulas capientes, tam jucundae refectionis auctori Deo gratias referamus, qui per singulos annos dulcissimi convivii participatione nos clementer exhilarat, dum beatissimi nobis Lebuini memoriam, annua natalis sui festivitate, tanquam panem angelorum ex ipso pietatis suae cophino prolatum repraesentat. Quod dum devote vescimur, salubriter esurimus, copiosissime pascimur, hilariter exultamus. His consequenter adjungitur habitudo mentis pulcherrima, fortitudo invicta, salus continua, contemptus mundi, appetitus coelestium, desiderium futurorum. Quocirca oportet nos perpendere, fratres quantae sint deliciae quae porriguntur, ut easdem sumere avido corde non differamus: quibus repleti nulla formidemus machinamenta hostium, nullo terreamur grandine saeculorum tempestatum. Atque, ut hoc divina miseratione assequi valeamus, hujus nobis sanctissimi viri exemplum sufficere posse credimus, qui inter adversa mundi et prospera, saevientis fortunae impetum, quemadmodum turris Sion, et porta Jerusalem praesidio angelico defensa, recussit, cassatisque ictibus machinarum in sempiternae fidei soliditate persistere meruit. Ad tantam vero perfectionem quibusdam bonorum naturalium gradibus ascendit, quibus quasi scalis evectus, terrena transiliens, coelorum alta feliciter penetravit. Denique in infantia sua Deo et hominibus charus exstitit; cumque esset ingenio docilis, animo mitis pauper spiritu, meritis dives, viris probatis certatim adnitentibus habitum religionis assumpsit, in quo ita Christo et Ecclesiae suae devotus effectus ut coaevos suos litterali sagacitate praecederet, majoribus officiosissime pareret, perfectorum imperiis tanquam a Deo datis vera humilitate praeditus acquiesceret. Porro in pueritiae annis, morum honestate sectatus est venerandam senum canitiem, innocentis vitae simplicitatem, doctrinae coelestis eruditione componens. Pubertatis autem spatia, non lascivientis animi voluptatibus effeminavit, sed potius rigore frugalitatis, et jugi laborum exercitio, rebellionem juventutis edomuit, castigans corpus suum et in servitutem redigens, ne forte, cum aliis praedicaret, ipse reprobus efficereretur. Hujus siquidem philosophiae nobilissimos professores, multos in sancta Ecclesia esse sciebat; inter quos felicis memoriae Willibrodum atque Bonifacium pontifices in vineae cultura Dominicae apprime laborasse audierat, ideoque animum Deo placitis operibus exercebat, ut quos habuerat in Christianitatis provectibus sociasset Patres, eosdem haberet in aeterna felicitate consortes. Enimvero quia tantorum familiae Christi luminarium sacra mentio nostris relationibus, ac si quidam venerandae lucis radius, illapsa est intermisso paululum superiore stylo, viros non sine mentis alacritate memorandos, dignis laudum praeconiis ad honorem Dei, prout possumus, extollamus; ut Lebuino nostro tanto crescat altior gloria, quanto se praecedentium probabilior fuisse dicitur vita: quando quidem nullis diverticulis ab eorum tramite declinavit, qui tantorum vestigia ducum summis nisibus fuerit exsecutus. Quapropter, cum illorum religiositas exprimitur, iste laudatur; cum horum studia praenotantur, iste totus depingitur; cum illorum praeliandi adversus potestates aereas certamina referunt, hujus triumphus evidenter exponitur. Atque ex hujusmodi conjecturis facile colligitur memoria priorum vitam illustrari sequentium: et augeri filiis honestatem, cum eosdem Patrum gloriose viventium fulcit auctoritas. Viros igitur, quos praemisimus, sanctos admodum fuisse non dubitamus, quorum alter confessione, alter martyrio in comitatum Agni suscipi meruit, habentque nunc haereditatem cum Christo, qui in hac vita nunquam passi sunt separari a Christo. Hos certe nobis imitabiles divina pietas condonavit, ut quem deterret a gladio manus violentae carnificis, magnum Willibrodum in divinae pacis quietudine Domino laudabiliter servientem, si possit, se aequiparet; qui autem se agonistis comparabilem existimat, sanctum Bonifacium fuso pro Christi amore sanguine subsequi non formidet. Quod si defuerit peremptoris atrocitas, ipse sibi manum divina rumphaea perarmet, ipse sibi spiritualiter, et persecutor efficiatur, et martyr, dummodo aut unius n pace munditiam, aut alterius in carnificio adipisci non negligat palmam. Sed his summotenus memoratis, repetenda est nobis historia, quam paulo ante nos omisisse perscripsimus: quae tamen penitus omissa non est, quia subinde se inter caetera animo huic semper inhaerente opposuit affectus distantis, nescio qua dulcedine delibutus dum superiora componeret reliquorum quidem digitis, Libuini autem jugiter corde conterunt. Sane quia de illo imprimis scriptitare decreverat, licet viros pretiosissimos repente in medium proferret, ab hujus tamen intuitu cogitantis intentio submoveri non potuit; quoniam bona quae de ipso dici queant ultro se offerunt, quae si quis omnia exponenda praesumeret, Tullianae, Plautinaeve eloquentiae floribus indigeret. Beatus igitur Lebuinus inter feros et semibarbaros hominum mores constitutus, agni innocentiam retinebat, memor Dominicae vocis quae dixerat se apostolos sicut agnos inter lupos missurum. Nec viro sancto defuit serpentina prudentia, dum si quis capiti suo, id est Christo, injuriam facere pertentaret, ille pro eo totum corpus indubitanter objiceret. Unde factum est ut in virtute Altissimi, ad divinum caput membra connecteret, utpote ut qui se inter ista medium quasi charitatis viscarium inserebat, infimoque summis copulans, infirmitatem humanam dignitati angelicae coaequare studebat. Sapiens plane architectus, qui coelestem aedificans domum, petram in fundamento locaverat, ne furentibus ventis, ne procellis aestuantibus, postremo ne impugnata totius adversitatis machinis virtutum consignatio laederetur. Petra autem erat Christus. Age ergo quisquis haec audire desideras, num tibi quidpiam videtur aut illa connexione salubrius, aut ista firmitate solidius, dum quod ibi copulatum est, nulla resolutione laxatur: quod hic fundatum est, nulla tempestate subvertitur. Quod si forte cuilibet monstruosis fabulis aurem accommodare vacat aut placet, invisum se veris relationibus hujusmodi vanitate demonstrans, poetarum deliramentis incumbere poterit, qui usque adeo praestigiosis figmentorum imaginationibus dementati sunt, ut ne ipsa quidem, quae interdum esse falsissima asserebant, falsa esse cognoscerent. Nos de sancto Dei Lebuino nihil mentitos esse testem habemus Ecclesiam, quae hujus beneficiis cumulata quam grandis apud Divinitatem meriti fuerit, crebris remediorum proventibus confitetur. Cui quidem ea quae de illo dicimus grata fore judicio est, quod legenti tantus assistat populus auditorum, ut compressum multitudinis etiam hi pertimescant, qui in tuto loco stare videntur, vixque in digressu aliquis inveniatur, qui non Deo gratias referat pro eo quod se patrocinium Lebuini audisse pariter et sensisse commemorat. Unde nobis adhuc vel pauca locuturis arbitramur neminem succensurum, quippe cum Spiritum Dei in ipso templum aedificasse, atque id sibi habitabile fecisse procedens sermo declamet. Idipsum vero inter matutinas laudes (ut credo) cantabitur, sed in lectione omitti non debuit, quo utriusque vocis ministerio quanti apud suos habeatur vir in Christo amabilis accipiat commendatum. Quod autem praemittitur tale est. Spiritus Sanctus (ut ait Scriptura) in corde viri justi habitat. Nam templum ipsius est anima ab omni iniquitate aliena, in quo non carnalis victima caeditur, sed spirituales hostiae offeruntur: nec fit ibi sola emundatio corporis, sed et remissio vera peccati et abolitio perpetuae mortis. Hoc templum dici et esse meruit beatus Lebuinus, cum praestante Domino a criminum fieret contagio mundus, per eum qui vivit et regnat in saecula saeculorum. Amen.

ENGLISH TRANSLATION

SERMON BY ST. RADBOUD ON ST. SWITBERT.

1. Dear brothers, we must be prepared for every good work and have willing hearts on the day of our special joy, in which the most blessed commemoration of our patron Switbert is to be made; first indeed to hear the mandates of divine law, and afterwards to strive to carry them out in deeds as much as we can, and thus finally be able to teach others. For this our Lord Jesus Christ did, of whom it is written: Jesus began to do and to teach (Acts I, 1). Otherwise, our teaching will be void and empty if we destroy what we have said by not acting. For what good is it to someone if he hears well but acts badly? Or what does it profit him if he shows others the way of feet but does not cease to err in the way of morals? Therefore, following the footsteps of our Redeemer, let us gladly hear any good; and having heard, let us complete it with worthy actions, and thus, approaching in order to instruct our neighbors, let us consult them with teachings and examples of good things. Therefore, whether it can be done with delay, let us recall to our memory the works of our Father, of whom we have spoken above: who in all that he taught first gave an example to his hearers from himself, nor did he ever say anything to be done in the Church other than what he himself preceded by doing. But that it may also be made clear to those who wish to imitate him, let his pleasing deeds to God, and all that is necessary for every hearer, be recited publicly, so that from them the people of Christ may receive edification and may always rejoice in the glorious prayers of such a man.

But since there are certain things hidden from us which only antiquity knows he did after God: indeed, it is proven that he came from the province of the Angles to our borders, the writings of the venerable Bede the priest should be presented, who in the Registers of the

Angles leaves behind this written account about this most holy man among other things.

2. At the time of Blessed Willibrord, the bishop of Trajectum, brothers, who were dedicated to the ministry of the word in Frisia, chose from their number a man modest in morals and gentle in heart, Switbert, to be their bishop. He was appointed by the most reverend Wilfrid, who, being driven from his homeland, was exiled in the regions of Mercia, at their request. For at that time there was no bishop in Kent, indeed after the death of Theodore, but not yet Berthwald, his successor, who had gone across the sea to be ordained at the seat of his bishopric. This Switbert, having received the episcopate, returned from Britain and shortly thereafter withdrew to the people of the Boructuarii, leading many of them to the way of truth by preaching. But after the Boructuarii were conquered, those who had received the word were scattered by the people of the ancient Saxons. The bishop himself sought Pippin, who, at the urging of his wife Blithrude, gave him a place of residence on the island of the Rhine, which in their language is called on the shore. There, having built a monastery, which his heirs possess to this day, he lived a very chaste life for some time, and there he closed his last day.

3. Therefore, we believe that no one doubts that these things, which have been discussed above about this most holy man, have been mentioned by Bede, unless perhaps someone such as he who, busy with other matters, either has not read that book where these things are written or has certainly neglected it while reading. However, we should not doubt at all that this man was exercised in all studies of the Christian religion, as he was worthy to be ordained a shepherd of Christ's flock among such precious lights of the Church of God, which shone wonderfully these days either among the Angles or among the people of Gaul. For unless he had been fully instructed in pastoral duty, no one would have believed him capable of guarding such a large flock of Christ. Moreover, unless he was in some way a veteran soldier, strong and undaunted in the contest of martyrdom, he would not have been established as the highest tribune of Christ in the army, nor

as the first centurion of divine law. However, having allegorically pre-explained these things, we must also morally open what the exercises are, by which we do not doubt that this illustrious soldier was invincible. This is indeed first demonstrated in pastoral duties, in which either a raging lion or a lurking wolf brings no small harm to the sheep of Christ: where if the pastor is vigilant, he either avoids ambushes or bravely repels the plunder, he will return safely with the flock to the Lord's folds. If, however, he, placed in daily readiness, never laid down his arms, but either repelled the enemy from the camp or rightly triumphed in open battle, he will thereafter rule most safely within the walls of the holy city.

4. Indeed, we do not ignore that the most blessed Switbert did both of these things. For while performing the office of a bishop in the Church, he either drew his brothers away from deceptive persuasions or recalled them from public contentions, excluding them from the flock of the Lord as a most fierce lion and as a most cunning wolf. When, however, he defended those pressed by the power of kings or tormented by any cruelty of princes with the sword of the word of God and the shield of faith from tyrannical persecution, he certainly led his soldiers back to camp unharmed as an excellent leader. Therefore, if you desire to know what were the arms of our leader in daily encounters, recognize them not as fabricated but plainly spiritual. For he was not burdened with iron but rather girded with faith, hope, and charity; holding the sling of David with his stone and striking the terrible Philistine in the forehead, rescuing all Israel from the danger of death. Moreover, do not think that he was ever accustomed to lay down such arms; he was adorned in peace with the same things with which he stood armed in war.

He was always humble, always gentle and mild, patient in adversity, modest in prosperity. He was also splendid in chastity, vigorous in abstinence, sober in watchfulness, and most steadfast in prayer. In judgment, he spoke equally, not personally; in compassion, he felt humanly, not harshly; he was not a seeker of others' possessions, but a most generous giver of his own; he pursued vice in man keenly, but embraced the man familiarly. His speech was as sweet as honey, his preaching exceedingly delightful, his banquet full of spiritual dishes, his companionship angelic; he rejected all evils as if they were deadly poisons; he cherished all goods as if they were the fragrances of paradise. Finally, if you wish to make a sort of epilogue; he was entirely perfect, and wholly filled with God. These were, brothers, the most blessed arms of our patron Switbert in adversity and prosperity: with these, he fought in every struggle and always prevailed everywhere. For his struggle was not against flesh and blood, but against principalities and powers, against the rulers of the darkness of this world, against spiritual wickedness in high places.

Let us therefore give thanks to Almighty God on this solemn day of this most holy bishop, praying together and asking that, whose glorious life we proclaim on earth, we may deserve to enjoy his patronage in heaven. Amen.

SERMON OF RADBOUD ON THE LIFE OF ST. VIRGIN AMELBERGA OF CHRIST.

1. Whenever, beloved brothers, we commemorate the memory of the saints of God for the praise and glory of His name, we rise from the graves of our sins. For then, in a way, our faith revives, and our voice is renewed with sweetness through the offices of our lips, and thus let what the Apostle says be in us: "Be renewed in the spirit of your mind, and put on the new man" (Eph. 4:23). For what else is it to die badly, to lie in a grave, and to stink, except to be polluted by the filth of sins? And what else is it to rise from this tomb, except to return to life, which is Christ, through confession and repentance? Indeed, we have many examples of such death in the Scriptures, which usually call those dead who never wish to repent from their sins; as it is in the Gospel: "Let the dead bury their dead" (Luke 9:60). For those who buried the bodies were not corporeally dead; but since they were wicked, and therefore dead, they buried those whom the death of the body had taken away from life. Therefore, let us also beware of the

losses of this death; rather, let us hasten to rise quickly from the graves of vices by the grace of Christ, so that we may deserve to live with Him in eternal bliss.

2. Therefore, let us praise the Lord our God in His saints, and let us in turn praise and honor them in Him, since to serve God and His saints is truly to live, and to remain in this at all times is to prudently avoid the snares of sins. Behold, however, today presents us with the most suitable time for this matter, in which we commemorate the memorable life of the paradoxical virgin Amalberga with an annual feast, who was most pleasing to God and men in this pilgrimage, both for the brilliance of her twin beauty and for the merit of her virgin chastity. She, when she was born of noble birth and because of her excessive bodily beauty was beloved by all, chose to adorn herself with the gems of virtues rather than with precious garments, and she decided to show herself to human eyes as vile and despicable, so that she might appear precious and most honorable to divine eyes. She did not use gold or pearls, because she knew that Christ, her bridegroom, had not used such things on earth; she did not love purple or fine linen, for she was not ignorant that many were drowned in the abyss because of such things. She did not delight in the murmurs of popular crowds, for she knew that a secret place was a suitable friend of sorrow.

3. Furthermore, having despised these things, she acted very differently; for, instead of relatives and friends of the world, she loved the poor of Christ; instead of gold and pearls, she adorned herself with the sayings of spiritual doctrine; instead of fine purple garments, she used ashes and sackcloth; instead of the popular crowd, which she utterly rejected, she continually stayed in the watch of the Lord's temples, praying and vigilantly remaining around the sacred altars. However, how and in what order she reached such a height of heavenly discipline cannot be passed over in silence because of her good example and the worthy proclamation of her merits. Indeed, this most chaste girl was in the inheritance of her fathers during the times of the Frankish princes, whom we can indeed call Carolingians from Charlemagne, who, because of multiple victories and his acceptance of stud-

ies in the Christian religion, alone among others earned the title to be rightly called great and most excellent.

4. In those days, as has been said, the holy and God-pleasing virgin Amelberga, her parents now deceased, was residing with her only brother, very religiously, in the possession that had come to her from the extensive inheritance of her ancestors near the river Scaldus, serving with fasting and prayers day and night, making many and very generous alms with the greatest joy, always having in mind that apostolic saying: "God loves a cheerful giver" (2 Cor. 9:7). And since she was so beautiful that she surpassed all others in her beauty, because of the prerogative of her most honorable body, she almost incurred the detriment of her chastity. For when her reputation reached the king of the province, namely Charles, at that time, he, continually captivated by her love, began to negotiate incessantly about marriage with her through messengers.

After he realized that his will was being entirely rejected by the blessed virgin, who had devoted herself to a better spouse, namely Christ, he attempted in every way to ensnare her through flattery and royal power, but he could not succeed through deceit and certain clandestine robberies. But she, in opposition to all these things, displayed the shields of prayers and the weapons of heavenly armor.

On a certain day, while the most blessed girl was sitting alone within her domestic walls, singing psalms as was her custom, a familiar boy suddenly burst in through the back door, proclaiming and announcing that the king was present with his attendants at the gates. Then she, forgetting nothing of herself, entered swiftly into the oratory that was attached to the house, where she immediately prostrated herself with a groan and tears in prayer, beseeching in a lamentable voice that the Lord would deliver her from imminent danger. Then indeed the king, excessively rash, entered the oratory after her and began to flatter her with many compliments, promising her temporal honors, so that he might make her yield to his persuasions. However, she, unwilling to abandon the spouse she had chosen, lay immobile, fixed to the ground as if she were held by any roots. After the king had used all his flattery (empty words) and saw that he was getting nowhere, he turned his royal authority into the most savage tyranny and, seizing her hand, attempted to drag her out violently. But since even then no one followed him, finally shaking off the girl's arm with great force and twisting it with all his might, he left her, breaking the bone of her virgin shoulder as if he had avenged himself.

Then she, being very tender, wept a little before the Lord because of the severe pain of her wound; however, she prayed until her spouse Christ was present, restoring her to perfect health. From that day on, she suffered no more worldly lovers but freely remained in the love of her spouse, our Lord Jesus Christ. O happy commerce! O exceedingly wise choice, where the king of the earth is despised for the Creator of heaven and earth, where God is loved for man, where celestial riches are sought for this clay! O most blessed virgin, if the nobility of your lineage harmed you much, or much more your spontaneous humility and the contrition of the flesh for God placed you? If the splendor of your beauty incurred danger, and the contempt of royal majesty crowned you with eternal glory. If for an hour passion saddened you, yet from that you obtained the companionship of martyrs and everlasting rest. Behold now you enjoy all that you desired in this life, since the king of kings and Lord of lords has desired your beauty, and you, O most august queen, stand at his right hand, surrounded by variety in golden garments.

Now therefore in you faith, hope, charity shine, humility reigns, patience triumphs, virginity glows, chastity shines, prudence discerns, temperance moderates, fortitude overcomes, justice judges, and, to make a summary, the military of all virtues is contained in you and from you. Therefore, in eternal beatitude, you behold ineffable goods, not only with the most blessed eyes do you see, and with the most fortunate hands do you hold, but also the remaining senses enjoy the same happiness. For with blessed ears you hear the heavenly organ, and with a joyful mouth you sing a new song, and with venerable nostrils you now enjoy everlasting fragrant delights. Thus, there will no longer be anything that causes you anxiety or brings you distress. Indeed, you have joy without sadness, delight without disgust, security without fear, peace without dissension, sweetness without bitterness, satisfaction without defect. Light shines for you without darkness, purity shines without pollution; you have complete rest, you possess life entirely, which neither allows you to grow weary, nor do you succumb to death.

What then is better? What is more pleasant? Earthly riches are either taken away by the wheel of fortune or extorted by the condition of mortality; however, heavenly treasures are made most desirable by their very perpetuity. You, O most blessed virgin, share these with the angels because of your celibate life; with the apostles, because of the Catholic faith; with the martyrs, because of the constancy of passion; with the confessors, because of holy innocence; with the virgins, because of special purity of body and soul; truly now, returning to your homeland beyond the thresholds, you partake by hereditary right, and you glory in your spouse Jesus Christ our Lord: through whom we pray and humbly ask that you do not cease to intercede for us with him, who has strengthened you in this mortality, so that you might overcome the earthly king with the glory of chastity, and surpass the prince of hell, the devil, with supreme holiness, through the help of him who, with the Father and the Holy Spirit, is glorified God, throughout all ages of ages. Amen.

HOMILY OF SAINT RADBOUD ON SAINT LEBWIN.

It often happens, dearest brothers, that among the feasts a delightful fable is pleasing to those who are dining, and the spirit oppressed by carnal foods is pursued by any hunger of fictions, while the mind, forgetting itself, at times, due to the repletion of the body, despises spiritual nourishment, craving more the appearance of vanities that please the ears of the flesh than the sweetness of heavenly doctrine, which refreshes the weary soul with true and lasting sweetness. However, we rejoice that in the present reading it happens quite differently, for the more solemnly we perceive this with the ear of the flesh, the more eagerly we consume it, and we do not doubt that the very same thing we take after the revered hunger creates a renewed hunger within us after the happy satisfaction.

Therefore, in order that it may shine more clearly what is promised (as it is said) to the spiritually famished through this kind of narration, let us now place on the heavenly table dishes more pleasing than all the delights of this world, from which, taking the most delightful feasts of eternal life, let us give thanks to God, the author of such joyful refreshment, who graciously enlivens us each year with the participation of the sweetest banquet, while representing to us the memory of the most blessed Lebuin, as if from the storehouse of His piety, presented like the bread of angels during the annual celebration of his birth. While we devoutly partake of this, we healthily hunger, we are abundantly nourished, we rejoice cheerfully. Consequently, there follows the most beautiful disposition of the mind, invincible strength, continuous health, contempt of the world, desire for the heavens, longing for the future. Therefore, we must consider, brothers, how great are the delights that are offered, so that we do not delay to take them with eager hearts: filled with these, we fear no machinations of enemies, we are not terrified by the hail of worldly tempests. And, that we may be able to attain this by divine mercy, we believe that the example of this most holy man can suffice for us, who, amidst the adversities of the world and the prosperity of fortune, repelled the onslaught of raging fortune, just as the tower of Zion and the gate of Jerusalem were defended by angelic protection, and, having withstood the blows of machines, deserved to persist in the solidity of eternal faith. Indeed, to such perfection he ascended by certain degrees of natural goods, by which, as if elevated by stairs, he successfully penetrated the heights of heaven, transcending earthly things. Finally, in his childhood, he was dear to God and men; and although he was naturally teachable, gentle in spirit, rich in merits, he eagerly took on the habit of religion, striving to be devoted to Christ and His Church, so that he would precede his peers in literary sagacity, serve his elders most dutifully, and humbly submit to the commands of the perfected, as if given by God. Moreover, in his childhood years, he pursued the venerable grayness of the elders with the honesty of morals, combining the simplicity of innocent life with the learning of heavenly doctrine. However, during the periods of adolescence, he did not indulge in the pleasures of a lascivious spirit, but rather subdued the rebellion of youth through the rigor of frugality and constant labor, chastising his body and leading it into servitude, lest, while preaching to others, he himself should become reprobate. Indeed, he knew that among the noblest professors of this philosophy, many were in the holy Church; among whom he had heard that the blessed memory of Willibrord and Boniface had labored particularly in the cultivation of the Lord's vineyard, and thus he exercised his mind in works pleasing to God, so that those whom he had had as companions in the advancement of Christianity would also be his partners in eternal happiness. Truly, because the sacred mention of such luminaries of Christ's family has interposed in our accounts, as if a ray of venerable light had descended, let us, with minds not without alacrity, extol those men worthy of commendation to the honor of God, as best we can, so that the glory of our Lebuin may grow higher, in proportion as the life of those preceding him is said to have been more probable: since he did not deviate from their path through any diversions, having followed the footsteps of such great leaders with utmost effort. Therefore, when their religiosity is expressed, this one is praised; when their studies are noted, this one is entirely depicted; when their struggles against the aerial powers are recounted, this one's triumph is evidently displayed. And from such conjectures, it is easily gathered that the memory of the former illuminates the life of the latter: and that the honor of the sons is increased, as the authority of the glorious living fathers supports them. Therefore, we do not doubt that the men we have mentioned were very holy, one of whom merited to be received into the company of the Lamb by confession, and the other by martyrdom, and they now have an inheritance with Christ, who in this life never suffered to be separated from Christ. Certainly, divine piety has granted us these to imitate, so that whoever is deterred by the sword of the violent hand of the executioner may aspire to be like the great Willibrord, who serves the Lord in the tranquility of divine peace; and whoever considers himself comparable to the athletes should not hesitate to follow the holy Boniface, who shed his blood for the love of Christ. But if the cruelty of the executioner should be lacking, let him arm himself with the divine spear, let him spiritually make himself both a persecutor and a martyr, provided that he does not neglect to attain the palm of one's purity or the other's martyrdom. But, having mentioned these things, we must return to the history, which we previously noted we had omitted: which, however, was not entirely omitted, because it has repeatedly interposed itself among other matters, with the mind always adhering to this affection, having been imbued with some sweetness while composing the higher things, while the fingers of the others indeed are left behind, but the heart of Libuin continually crushes. Indeed, because he had primarily decreed to write about him, although he suddenly brought forth the most precious men in the midst, yet the intention of considering this could not be removed; since the good things that can be said about him offer themselves voluntarily, which, if anyone presumed to expose all, would require the flowers of Tullian or Plautinian eloquence. Therefore, blessed Lebuin, established among the fierce and semi-barbarous manners of men, retained the innocence of a lamb, mindful of the Lord's voice which said He would send His apostles as lambs among wolves. Nor did the holy man lack serpentine wisdom, for if anyone were to attempt to do injury to his head, that is, Christ, he would undoubtedly offer his whole body for Him.

Wherefore it came to pass that in the power of the Most High, he connected the members to the divine head, as one who inserted himself in the midst of these things as if in the bowels of charity, coupling the lowest with the highest, and striving to equate human weakness with angelic dignity. Truly a wise architect, who, while building the heavenly house, had placed the rock as the foundation, lest it be harmed by raging winds, by surging storms, and ultimately, lest the establishment of the virtues be injured by the engines of all adversity. The rock, however, was Christ. Therefore, whoever desires to hear this, does anything seem to you either more healthful than that connection, or more solid than that firmness, while what is joined there is not loosened by any resolution: what is founded here is not overthrown by any tempest. But if perhaps anyone is free to lend an ear to monstrous fables or finds pleasure in them, demonstrating that such vanity is opposed to true accounts, he will be able to indulge in the deliriums of poets, who have become so mad with the prestidigitation of their imaginations that they do not even recognize what they sometimes assert to be most false as being false. We have the Church as a witness that we have not lied about the holy man Lebuin, which, being enriched by these benefits, confesses how great it has been in merit before God, through the frequent fruits of remedies. Indeed, it is judged that what we say about him will be pleasing, since such a great multitude of listeners stands by the reader, that even those who seem to stand in a safe place fear the crowd, and scarcely can anyone be found in the digression who does not give thanks to God for the fact that he recalls having heard and felt the patronage of Lebuin. Hence, we deem that no one will be angry with us, even if we speak a few words, since the Spirit of God has built a temple in him, and the proceeding discourse proclaims that it has made him habitable. Indeed, the same will be sung during the morning praises (as I believe), but it should not have been omitted in the reading, so that by the ministry of both voices, the worth of the man beloved in Christ may be commended among his own. What is premised is as follows: The Holy Spirit (as Scripture says) dwells in the heart of a just man. For his temple is the soul alien to all iniquity, in which no carnal victim is slain, but spiritual sacrifices are offered: nor is there merely the cleansing of the body, but also true remission of sin and the abolition of eternal death. This temple is worthy to be called and to be the blessed Lebuin, when, by the Lord's grace, the world was cleansed from the contagion of crimes, through him who lives and reigns forever and ever. Amen.

This work was produced in association with:

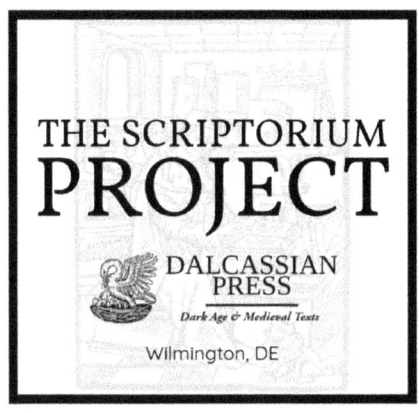

www.ingramcontent.com/pod-product-compliance
Lightning Source LLC
LaVergne TN
LVHW061049070526
838201LV00074B/5240